# DOG M🐾M

## A LOVE STORY

# DOG M🐾M

## A LOVE STORY

ISABEL SERNA

Library of Congress Cataloging-in-Publication Data is available.

ISBN 978-1-5235-0810-5

Author photo: Paola Paladini Pet Photography

Workman books are available at special discounts when purchased in bulk for premiums and sales promotions as well as for fund-raising or educational use. Special editions or book excerpts can also be created to specification. For details, contact the Special Sales Director at the address below, or send an email to specialmarkets@workman.com.

Workman Publishing Co., Inc.
225 Varick Street
New York, NY 10014-4381

workman.com

Printed in China
First printing August 2020

10 9 8 7 6 5 4 3 2 1

To Charlie, who made me the craziest of dog moms, and to Olafo, Pulga, Max, Moncho, Rosie, Zuzu, Pepe, Yako, Ramón, Corbin, Lola, Maga, Mowgli, and all the dogs who have shared their love and souls with me.

To Juangui, mami, papi, Angie, Dani, and Noa: You are my world. To the wonderful people at Workman: Thank you for your unconditional support and trust.

"Because of the dog's joyfulness, our own is increased."
—Mary Oliver

# DOG MOM

noun ( / dȯg / mäm )

1. A woman who is obsessed with her dog and treats him/her as her child.

2. A woman whose everyday life revolves around her dog.

3. A woman whose love for her dog surpasses her love for most people.

# TYPES OF DOG MOMS

THE LAZY MOM

THE ACTIVE MOM

THE TEACHER MOM

## THE SELFIE MOM

## THE SOCIAL MOM

## THE GADGET MOM

# fun fact

WHEN DOGS GAZE INTO OUR EYES, OUR BODIES (AND THEIRS!) ARE FLOODED WITH OXYTOCIN, THE LOVE HORMONE THAT CEMENTS OUR BONDS WITH OTHERS. ♥

# A DAY IN THE LIFE OF A DOG MOM

Wake Up

Morning Walk

Good Night

Cuddle time

Get Ready

I PROMISE I'LL BE BACK ASAP!

Say Goodbye

Work

Come home

Dinnertime

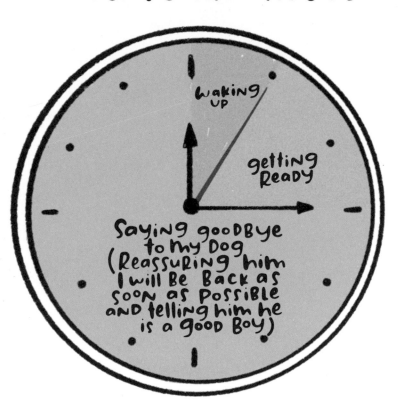

LOOK AT MY BABY!
<albums
select

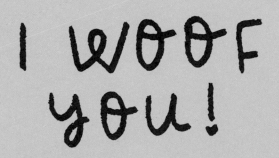

# NORMAL DOG MOM

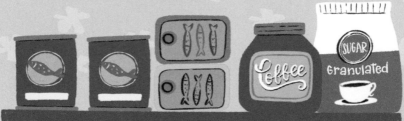

# CRAZY DOG MOM

YOU KNOW YOU'RE A **CRAZY DOG MOM** WHEN...

YOU HAVE FULL CONVERSATIONS WITH YOUR DOG.

hi, sweetie! I missed you so much!
Did you miss me too? I'm so sorry I left you but I already told you mommy has to work to buy you all the treats!
How was your day?
I bet you're hungry!
I'll make your food and then we'll go for a walk!

# THINGS MY DOG WANTS TO EAT

- Shoes
- Grass
- Literal Trash
- My Food
- His Organic, Gluten-Free, Non-GMO, Grain-Free, Protein-Rich, Human-Grade, Nutritious & Super-Expensive Food

# INSIDE THE PURSE of a CRAZY DOG MOM

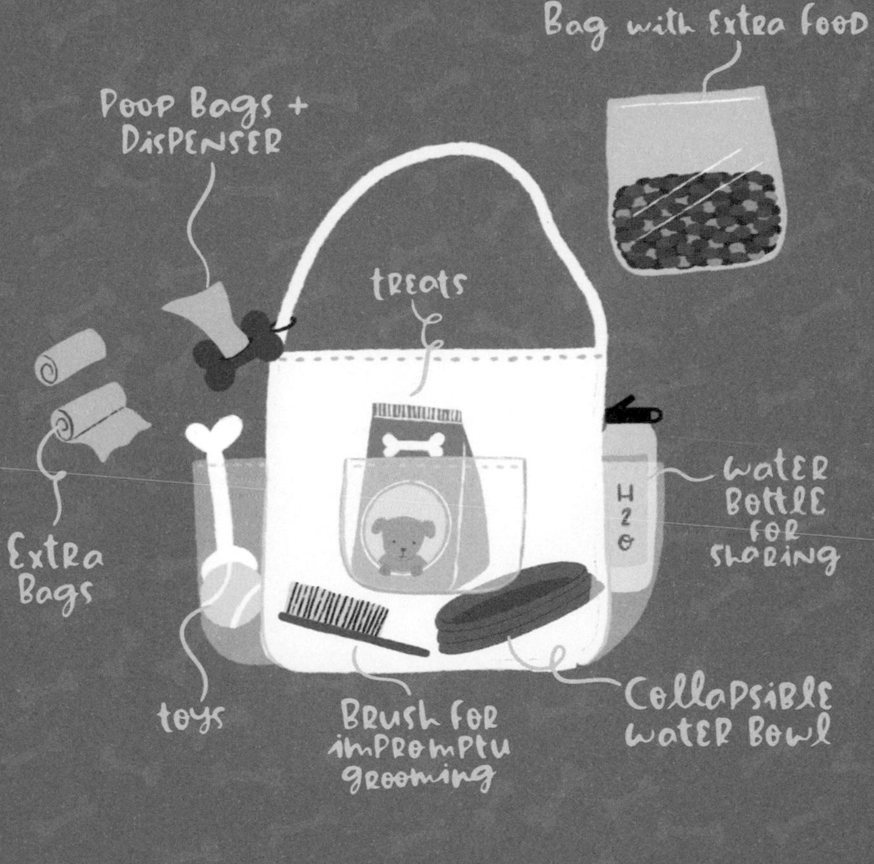

BUSINESSWOMAN
LEONA HELMSLEY
WAS KNOWN AS THE
"QUEEN OF MEAN",
BUT HAD A SOFT SPOT
FOR DOGS — SHE LEFT
$12 MILLION IN HER
WILL TO TROUBLE,
HER WHITE MALTESE,
AND A CLAUSE IN THE
WILL SPECIFIED THAT
TROUBLE SHOULD BE BURIED
NEXT TO HER IN THE
HELMSLEY MAUSOLEUM.

fun fact

JUST LIKE HUMAN FINGERPRINTS, NO TWO DOGS' NOSEPRINTS ARE the SAME.

# YOU KNOW YOU'RE A CRAZY DOG MOM WHEN...

you match
outfits with
YOUR DOG.

I Just want
to WORK HARD
to GIVE MY dog
THE LIFE
HE DESERVES.

# A DOG MOM'S FAVORITE

THE KISS ATTACK

THE CRADLE

THE BUTT SCRATCH

THE BELLY RUB

# PETTING TECHNIQUES

THE CHEEK GRAB

THE HEAD SCRATCH

THE EAR PULL

THE MASSAGE

YOU KNOW YOU'RE A
**CRAZY DOG MOM**
WHEN...

109K
FOLLOWERS

ADD FRIEND

LOUIE the GREAT

YOUR
DOG
has his
OWN
SOCIAL
MEDIA
account.

In ancient China, people kept warm by putting DOGS up their sleeves.
brrr

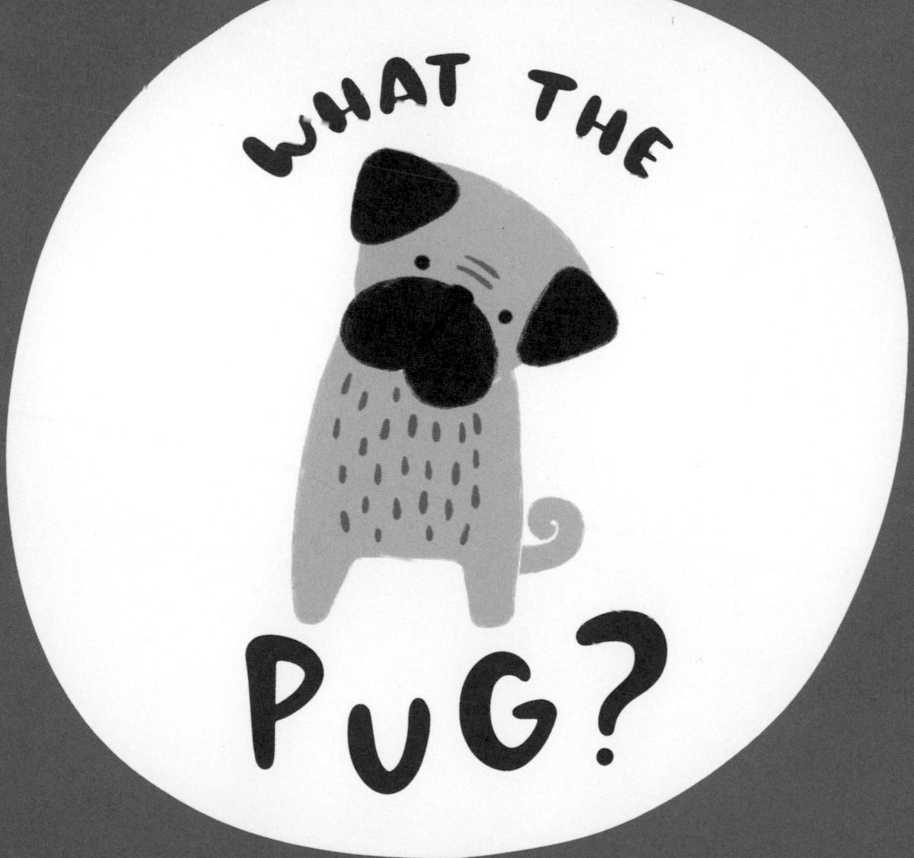
WHAT THE
PUG?

BATH TIME
BEFORE
BECOMING A DOG MOM

# BATH TIME
[AFTER]
## BECOMING A DOG MOM

SORRY i WAS late. MY DOG WAS doing SOMETHING REALLY CUTE !

YOU KNOW YOU'RE A
CRAZY DOG MOM
WHEN...

YOU THROW
BIRTHDAY PARTIES
FOR YOUR DOG.

"DOGS? What? DOGS? These are my FUR CHILDREN, and they always make me feel HAPPIER AND more human."

—OPRAH WINFREY

EXPECTATION

# Pardon my Frenchie

you plan
your Dog's
Halloween costume
months in advance.

CANIS

SIRIUS

MAJOR

SIRIUS, THE "DOG STAR," IS LOCATED IN THE DOG CONSTELLATION CANIS MAJOR, AND IS THE BRIGHTEST STAR IN OUR SKY.

# DOG MOM BINGO

| | | | | |
|---|---|---|---|---|
| You celebrate your dog's birthday | You cook for your dog | You stay home with your dog | You have too many treats and toys | You have puppy-proofed your house |
| You never have any privacy | Your dog has had a professional photo shoot | You call your dog your "furry baby" | You have too many nicknames for your dog | You've bought your dog a puppuccino |
| You have SO many pictures of your dog | You buy souvenirs for your dog when you're away | 🐾 | You pet every dog you see | You own a dog teepee |
| You own a DOG MOM bumper sticker, T-shirt, mug, or jewelry | You have the vet on speed dial | You plan dog-friendly activities every week | You watch your dog sleep | You Netflix and chill with your dog |
| You are always rushing home to see your dog | You dress your dog | Your clothes and furniture are covered in dog hair | You create songs for your dog | You have moved homes for your dog |

# Dogs

~~Diamonds~~ are a girl's best friend.

YOU KNOW YOU'RE A **CRAZY DOG MOM** WHEN...

you only go to DOG-FRIENDLY PLACES.

SCOTTSDALE, ARIZONA, is the most PET-FRIENDLY city in the US.

Queen Elizabeth II has owned more than 30 CORGIS in her life. On her 18th birthday, she was given a corgi named SUSAN (whom she even brought on her honeymoon). Ever since, her pet corgis have often accompanied her on her travels and to Royal events.

LIFE
is
RUFF

**fun fact**

THE SECOND SATURDAY OF MAY IS Dog mom's Day!

# BEFORE VACATION

You LEAVE A LONG LIST OF CARE INSTRUCTIONS FOR YOUR DOG SITTER.

THE snuggle IS real

FOOD POISONING

STRANGERS

ONCOMING TRAFFIC

THUNDERSTORMS

THE VACUUM

 THINGS that SCARE MY DOG

YOU KNOW YOU'RE A **CRAZY DOG MOM** WHEN...

YOU WERE EMOTIONAL AT YOUR DOG'S PUPPY SCHOOL GRADUATION.

# dog stars

LASSIE

HACHIKŌ

TOTO

SNOOPY

# RIN-TIN-TIN

was the
FIRST
Hollywood
dog star.

RIN-TIN-TIN

RIN-TIN-TIN

He appeared
in
27 films.

# fun fact

NEARLY 50% OF PEOPLE ARE MORE EXCITED TO SEE _THEIR DOG_ THAN TO SEE FAMILY OVER THE HOLIDAYS.

## YOU KNOW YOU'RE A CRAZY DOG MOM WHEN...

happy HOWLIDAYS!

YOUR HOLIDAY CARDS ALWAYS INCLUDE YOUR DOGS.

YOU LOVE WATCHING YOUR DOGS UNWRAP THEIR PRESENTS.

I LOVE YOU FUREVER

A DOG MOM'S ULTIMATE DREAM

# TO BE *Smothered* BY PUPPIES

Isabel Serna is the founder of Black Lamb Studio, a Miami-based design studio with a focus on colorful patterns, illustration, and product design.

She is formally trained as an industrial designer, and her work can be found on textiles, home goods, wrapping paper, stationery, and various printed media. She has collaborated with brands such as Kate Spade, Anthropologie, Hallmark, Huggies, Mixbook, Travelpro, and Figo Fabrics.

She lives with her husband, Juan, and her French bulldog, Charlie, in Miami, Florida.